Lindsay Kelley
December 7   1951

SONG OF
THE SEASONS

SONG OF
THE SEASONS

by

Addison Webb

Illustrated by Charles L. Ripper

New York, 1950

William Morrow & Company

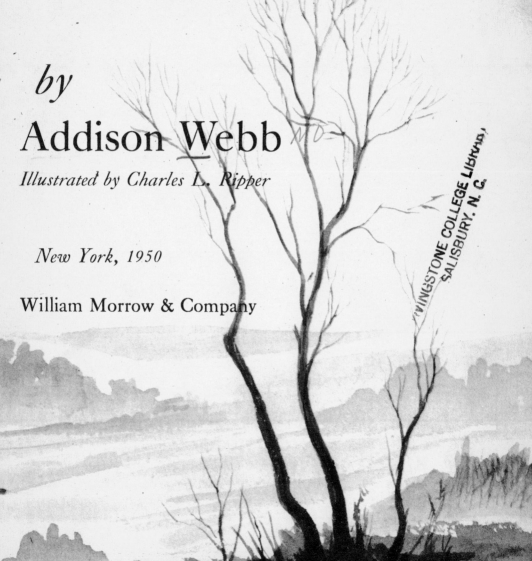

There are four seasons in every year. They are spring, summer, autumn, and winter. Each one is different from the others. The animals of the air and of the land and of the water act differently in each of them.

Springtime is the season for babies. Summer is the time for learning. Autumn is the season for feasting. Winter is the time for rest. In each season nature is different.

This is the story of the seasons, of how they change and of how the changes affect the animals.

Spring

Spring is the season when nature awakens.
The streams that were locked up for the winter
with ice are free again and ripple and gurgle along
their way. The sap flows through the trees and
wakes up the resting buds. They unfold and let
the leaves out. The flowers begin to bloom.
Green grass creeps up through the dry dead
growth. The world that seemed so lifeless begins
to show life once more.

The animals that slept through the winter wake up. The birds return from the south. The work of the year is about to begin again. Everyone is busy.

The sun rises earlier and sets later. It melts the snow and warms the earth and the water. Millions of little drops of water soak into the hard ground and soften it. Soon it is mud, and the prisoners underneath work their way up. The earthworms plow through. The seeds burst and the plants come up. The pussy willows burst out of their warm winter coats and show off their blossoms. The skunk cabbage pokes its hooded head out of the marshlands.

Living creatures wriggle up through the ponds. Things stir in the mud and in the puddles and on the shores. They trill and chirrup and sing. The air is filled with a musical jingling.

Little frogs cry "Peep-peep" in a high shrill
voice. Big ones reply "Croak-croak" in deep
throaty notes. They call back and forth to each
other day and night without pause.

Nature is awakening.

The bees that clung together all winter to keep warm break up their clusters and go outdoors for a flight. The baby bees buzz as loud as they can. The queen bee begins to lay eggs. Soon she will lay as many as three thousands eggs a day.

Sap flows through the trees. The blossoms fill with nectar. This is the spring honey flow.

The worker bees begin their work of the year.

A hive needs many workers in this season to bring in the honey flow. That is why, in the springtime, the queen bee is busy laying thousands of eggs.

Three thousand eggs weigh as much as the queen who lays them. So in one day a queen can lay her own weight in eggs. The queen is able to do this only because the worker bees take good care of her. Every time a worker returns to the hive from the fields, she greets her queen with a lick and gives her a taste of nectar.

Over a hundred thousand workers go in and out of the hive every hour. So every hour the queen bee gets over a hundred thousand mouthfuls of nectar. That is why she can lay so many eggs. She has a busy life but a tasty one.

Each new day the sun rises a little earlier and shines on the earth a little longer. Each new day the earth grows a little warmer. As the earth warms, it warms the layer of air directly above it. This warm layer of air rises. A cool layer rushes in to take its place. This movement of one layer of air rising and another layer rushing in to take its place creates a wind.

The birds that went south for the winter now have a way of getting back—they can ride the

wind. All a bird need do is to get aboard a layer of air that is going his way and be careful not to fall into a layer of air that is rushing back. If a bird is careless and gets caught in a crosscurrent, he can sprain a wing.

The birds return to their old homes by riding the wind. If a home is damaged, the mother bird repairs it. If the home is damaged beyond repair, she builds a new one.

13

Some build up high.

Others build on the earth.

Some birds build a home under the earth.

The mother bird generally does the work. The father bird sits around and sings to her while she builds. Sometimes he brings her a twig or some dry grasses or a mouthful of mud.

The mother bird lays the eggs. Sometimes the father bird sits on them. He is a very good sitter.

The young hatch out and call for food. They grow on it and call loudly for more. They are soon big and noisy.

Down at the pond the mother frogs and toads lay thousands of eggs and set them adrift on the water. The father toads sit in the shallow puddles up to their elbows and sing. The bullfrogs drift among the cattails and sing. The peepers hide in the shore grasses and sing.

Nature is awake again. The old generation is singing to the new.

The pond is filling up with polliwogs.

The mother crayfish lays her eggs too. She glues them to her rear feet. There they stick, underneath her, and wherever she goes she takes along her family of eggs. She moves along with hundreds of eggs hanging from her.

In time the babies hatch out. They cling to the mother crayfish's feet until they are strong enough to stand on their own.

For two weeks she goes about with her children

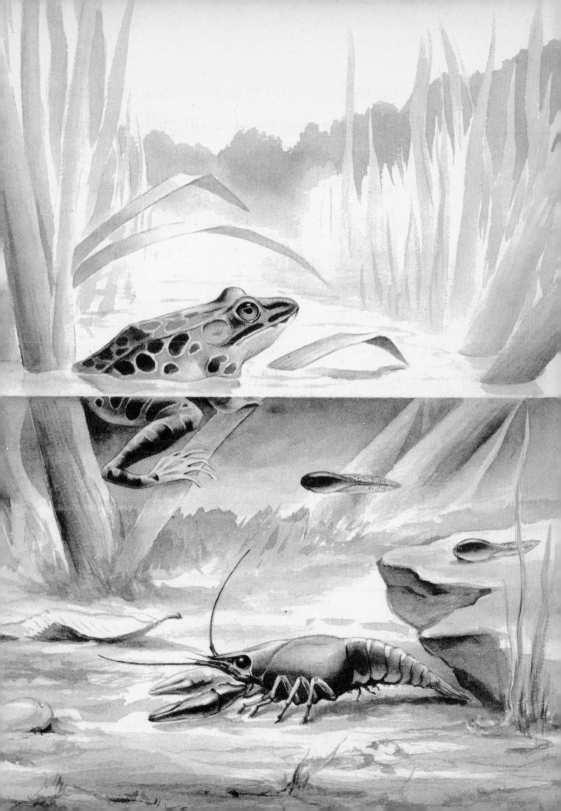

hanging onto her. Her eyes move in and out and in all directions. She watches carefully for things that she can eat and for things that can eat her. She cannot turn her head to look, because she has no neck. As she moves along the bottom of the pond, the mother crayfish watches for little fish near their nests.

Fish build nests for their eggs. The bass and the bullheads and the minnows hollow out holes in the mud or under big stones. There the mother fish deposits her eggs, and a layer of ooze flows over them and hides them.

The father fish is the builder. With a wriggle of his tail he pushes his head against the spot where he is digging. If stones are in the way, he pushes them out with his snout. If the stones are too big, other male fish help him to move them. But if his helpers linger around after the job is finished, he drives them away.

Some fish prefer a nest of stone to one of mud. They build with pebbles and with rocks. They push them together into a heap, or fetch them by mouth and heap them up into piles. The eggs slip in between the pebbles. Ooze and gravel drift over them and hide them from view.

Some fish eggs never have a nest. Pike and pickerel, for example, scatter their eggs among water plants. There they stick to stems and leaves until they hatch.

Eggs hatch in the springtime. Life in the pools

and in the streams is renewed. The world of fish is filled with babies again.

The father fish loses the beautiful colors he grew on his head and on his fins at the start of the season. Back again in his old colors, he doesn't look like such a handsome fish any more. The mother fish pays no attention to him except, perhaps, to snap at him when he crosses her path.

The animals on dry land build homes in the springtime and have babies, too. If there is an enemy about, they move and build elsewhere.

The mother squirrel gathers old leaves and stuffs them into a hole in a tree until it is well filled. Then she arranges them neatly. It is her new home. She lines it with thousands of small soft hairs. She pulls them out of her own tail, one by one. This makes a very comfortable bed for the babies.

Sometimes the mother squirrel stuffs her leaves into an old bird's nest in a treetop and shapes them into a home. Sometimes she prepares several such homes and moves about from one to another.

When a new home is ready, the mother squirrel carries her babies to it, one at a time. She holds them in her mouth by the skin of the belly. The babies put their little paws around her head and hold on tight.

From the new home they look out on the world about them until they are ready to go out into it themselves. If their father passes by, they scream. He left home before they were born and

they do not recognize him. To them, their father is a stranger who runs after their mother up and around the trees. They do not trust him.

Their mother made a home for them and furnished it with hairs out of her own tail. She brought them bugs and grubs and other good food. She fed them and protected them. They wish she would not run around with this stranger.

Some squirrels raise their children under the

ground. The chipmunk is such a squirrel. Down
under the earth the chipmunks have nurseries
and bedrooms and storerooms and spare rooms.
Many a chipmunk has an apartment of ten rooms.
Some have even more.

Each spring the mother chipmunk digs another
room or two and connects them with those she
already has. A tunnel leads into every home and
other tunnels lead out of it. Every room is con-

nected by tunnels. Some chipmunk homes have as many as forty feet of tunnels.

The chipmunk is small and timid. She is always on the run. Anything, or even nothing, frightens her. That is why she stays near her home. It has a front entrance to rush down and back doors to rush out of and tunnels to race along and rooms to hide in. Each room has an entrance and an exit and tunnels to get in by and tunnels to go

out by. For a chipmunk must always be ready to run away from danger, even when there is none.

To dig a chipmunk home is hard work. The diggings must not be piled up around the entrance or the exits. They must be patted tightly into the tunnel walls or carried away. The entrance and the exits must be well hidden. They must be large enough to rush down quickly and small enough to keep out an intruder.

A well-built chipmunk home must be below the frost line and below the heat line. It must be warm there when it is cold outside and cool when it is hot.

Every spring the mother chipmunk has a family of babies and raises them in such a home until they are old enough and bold enough to venture outdoors and dig a home for themselves.

The opossum's babies are among the smallest in the world. When born, they measure a half inch or less. They have no hair nor hide.

Opossum babies would be cold and uncomfortable in a nest, so the mother opossum carries them about in a warm fur-covered pouch on her underside.

If enemies pursue her, she rolls up around this pocket and plays dead. If they push her, she does not move. If they bite her, she does not cry out. She just lies still and waits for the danger to go away. She is very brave.

As soon as the children are big enough, they crawl out of their mother's pouch and climb onto her back. That is a very daring excursion. They grip their mother's hair firmly with their toes and pull themselves along till they reach the top of her. There they cling tightly as she travels along. They do not want to be unseated as their mother bumps over logs and up trees and along limbs.

The mother opossum bends her tail back over her back. The children grab it with their own tails and hang on. When they get tired, they crawl back into her pouch and go to sleep.

The mother opossum's tail is a very handy

piece of equipment. She can use it to steady the children on a ride. She can wrap it around bunches of leaves and gather them into piles. She can hang from a limb with it, head down, and swing.

The mother opossum likes to sleep all day. At night she eats. Her children learn to live in the same style.

There are a great many opposums in the world and chipmunks, too, and squirrels; but there are a great many more rabbits. They are everywhere.

Rabbits wander across the roads and in and out of the shrubbery in search of some other rabbit to keep company with. They sit near each other all day under an overhanging bush and twitch their noses and whisk their whiskers.

In the evening they go out together to nibble tender grasses. They nibble all through the night.

When morning comes, they return to their nooks under the overhanging bushes and again spend the day twitching their noses and whisking their whiskers. Millions of rabbits all over the country-side do just that and nothing else all day long: twitch, twitch; whisk, whisk.

When a mother rabbit is going to have her babies, she orders her friend to leave. She knows that some male rabbits kill the babies. If she has more than one friend around, she tells them all to go. If they do not obey her promptly, she stamps her front feet in anger. Then she rushes at them and bites off mouthfuls of their fur. Her

friends scurry off and wander across the roads and in and out of the shrubbery in search of another rabbit to keep company with.

The countryside is full of wandering male rabbits in the springtime. They go from friend to friend, only to be driven off again each time. That is why there are always rabbits wandering about the countryside.

The mother rabbit prepares the nest. It isn't much of a home, just a shallow hole in some sheltered spot where the father will not find it.

All day long the mother sits near the nest and watches it. If an intruder comes around, she drives him away. She will even go after the father if he dares to come around for a look at his children. That is why, in the springtime, he sits under a bush twitching noses and whisking whiskers with a new friend.

Foxes are different. They go off in pairs and together they select a shelter for their babies. Some fox couples look for a hollow log or a hole under an old tree, filled with leaves. Others look for a den under the ground. If the place they select is already occupied by another animal, they drive him out.

Foxes are not builders; they want a ready-made home. The only work they will willingly do for a home is to eat the occupant already in it.

They want a territory all to themselves, so they look for a place in which no other fox has settled. As long as they live there, they drive off any other fox that tries to move in.

For the beaver, springtime is the time to begin work again. The mother beaver will have babies and she wants a bed for them. The father can sleep on the bare floor, but the children must

have something softer. The father beaver must prepare a mattress for them out of tender twigs and grasses.

Soon the spring floods will come. The murmuring brooks will turn into roaring rushing

streams. The beaver must patch his dam before
that happens or else the rushing waters will wash
it away. He must strengthen it with sticks and
stones. He must add logs, and heavy rocks to
hold them in place. He must pile on branches

and brush, and sod to plaster them together. He must make his dam bigger and better than ever.

Some beaver dams become so high and so thick and so strong that horses can use them as a bridge.

Sometimes the father beaver cannot do all this work alone. He invites his relatives to help him with it. He whistles for his brothers and his uncles and his aunts. They come in the moonlight and help until the work is finished. Then he helps his relatives when they need him.

When the woodchuck gets up in the spring, he is thin and hungry and lonesome.

He was covered with thick layers of fat when he dug in for the winter. It filled his coat so full no more fat could fit into it. He was so fat he could not run. He could hardly walk. No wonder people called him "chuck," meaning "little fatty."

He was a very sleepy little animal when he went to bed for the winter. He slept right through into the spring and never got up to eat.

Now, in springtime, the woodchuck is thin and hungry and lonesome. He sniffs at the tunnels around him. He dug many of them himself. Others were dug by his brothers and his sisters and other relatives.

He sets off on a tour of discovery. He would like to find his old friends. Also he would like to find a mate; he has been alone too long. So he wanders from tunnel to tunnel and sniffs.

Sometimes he wakes up another woodchuck who growls and grinds his teeth in rage. Then he hurries along to the next tunnel. Sometimes he finds that an opossum has moved in, or a rabbit or a skunk. Then he hurries along to the next tunnel.

In time he finds the mate he is looking for.

On his tour of discovery he has met many animals. They realize that the woodchucks are awake and that it is spring. The streams are free of ice and are rippling and gurgling along their way. The birds are back from the south. Life is wriggling in the ponds and it is time again for babies.

For the woodchucks are awake. Spring has come.

Summer

Summer is the season for learning.

The baby birds learn to fly and to care for themselves. The baby animals learn to walk and to run and to care for themselves. They all play in the sunshine or in the moonlight and have a very good time.

By the end of the summer they are grown-up, and then they take care of themselves, forever after. They are educated. They have been gradu-

41

ated from their mother's watchful care and they are on their own.

The world is covered with beautiful flowers. The plants manufacture foodstuffs. They make sugars and starches and other good things. The leaves and the flowers feed on these foodstuffs and grow to full size. Some grow so fast you can almost see them grow.

Other living things feed on these plants, and still other forms of life, in turn, feed on them. There is always something about, eating some-

thing else. Everything is very busy, either running after or running away from something else.

The bees visit the flowers for pollen grains. They gather loads of them and pack them into the baskets on their hind legs.

Apple blossoms supply a pale yellow pollen. The baby bees have it at mealtimes, dipped in honey. The pollen from apricot, peach, and nectarine blossoms is brownish yellow. From asparagus it is pinkish-red, and from dandelion blossoms it is orange. There are pollen grains of every color. The young bees get nicely colored meals.

The bees also visit flowers for honey. They get a fine white honey from apple blossoms and from clover. They get a white honey, also, from milkweed, alfalfa, basswood, raspberry, and cotton blossoms. When the basswood is in bloom, it is full of buzzing bees. It sounds like a singing tree.

Honey from the star thistle blossom is light green. It is sea green from the gooseberry bush and from the sycamore tree. The sumac tree gives an amber honey and so do goldenrod, marigold, magnolia, and the royal palm. Buckwheat gives

the darkest honey of all. It is so dark that sometimes it looks almost black.

Summer is the time of song. Everything is in
full tune. Singers and drummers and violinists
make music. The trees and the bushes and the
grasses and the weeds are alive with musicians.
Some fiddle, others scrape their sides or slap their
stomachs. The world is full of sounds.

The katydids tell each other whether they did
or didn't. The mosquitoes buzz. The frogs croak.
The cicadas sing.

The young birds listen to these musicians and
chirp with joy when their father brings one home
in his beak.

The young bears wander down to the pond.
Something down there is croaking "Gar-rumph,
gar-rumph," and something else is answering
"Jug-o-rum, jug-o-rum." Perhaps it will be some-

body to play splash with. Perhaps it will be somebody to roll around with in the soft grass. Young bears love to splash and to wrestle and to chase each other up trees.

If they play on after the mother bear calls them, she will punish them, but she will not permit their father to lay a paw on them.

If a grizzly comes along, all the other bears get out of his way. If he snarls, they run. If he roars, they climb a tree—up to the very top. The mother bear climbs up, too. So does the father bear. Sometimes a tree is full of frightened bears and their cubs.

The grizzly is king of the bears. When he stands up on his hind legs, he is twelve feet tall. He is so strong he can kill a big bull with one blow. But he can't climb a tree.

The pond is full of young frogs. The male frog

sits around on a lily pad in the warm sun and waits for the little ones to pass his way. Then he gulps them down, whatever they are, even if they are his own brood. The female frog floats about. She, too, is very fond of her children for breakfast, lunch, or supper.

There are all kinds of frogs down at the pond. There are cricket frogs and peepers and leopard frogs and pickerel frogs and green frogs and wood frogs and bullfrogs. They all sit around, and wait for something to pass by that they can gulp.

The greatest gulper of them all is the bullfrog. He can gulp down any of the other frogs. When he would like something to gulp, he croaks "Gar-rumpf." After he has gulped it, he croaks "Jug-o-rum."

Many other animals pass the summer at the

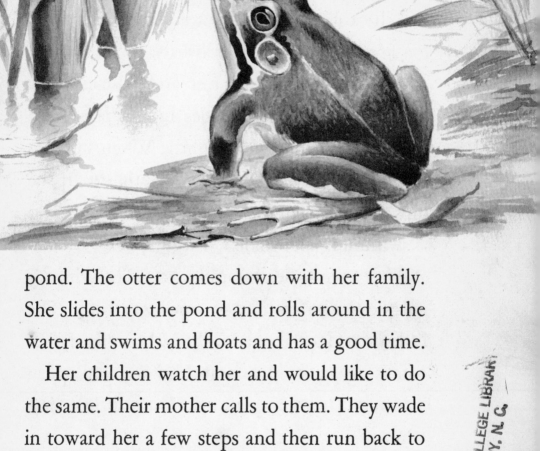

pond. The otter comes down with her family.
She slides into the pond and rolls around in the
water and swims and floats and has a good time.

Her children watch her and would like to do
the same. Their mother calls to them. They wade
in toward her a few steps and then run back to
land again. They are afraid.

The father otter catches a frog and brings it
out. He wants them to know that the pond is

51

full of interesting things. The frog jumps back into the water. The young otters scramble in after it a few steps and then rush back to land again.

Their mother comes out and nudges them onto her back. Then she slides into the pond with them. They cling to her tightly. When she dips under a little way, they cling even tighter. If she dips under too far, they grab for their father, who is swimming alongside.

After a while he dips under, too. Then there is no one to cling to and no one to grab for. The little otters kick about wildly. When their father comes up again, they grab him and get up on his back. They complain to him in little crying whimpers.

The father otter is a wise teacher. He holds them up. He lends them courage till their own comes back.

A young porcupine knows everything he ever will know almost as soon as he is born. He does not need teaching. But nobody likes him except his mother. She thinks he is wonderful.

His eyes are open. His teeth stick out. He is covered with a coat that has thirty thousand little needles sticking out of it. He can toddle about and swing his tail and stab anything within reach. No other one-day-old baby in the woods is his equal.

By the time he is two days old he can climb a tree. If his mother grunts to him, he grunts back promptly. If he grunts first, she gives him a drink and licks his nose.

But he isn't popular with anyone besides his mother. Nobody else is pleased with the noise he can make. If he grunts at a stranger, the stranger runs away. If he goes up a tree, everybody else

gets out of it. If he smacks his lips loudly over a tasty piece of bark, no one looks up to see what he is enjoying. If he throws down some tender green twigs, no one hurries over to feed on them. Even a hunter does not want his hide.

So from the time he is a little fellow two days old, he sits up in a tree all alone and chews bark sweetened with sap and smacks his lips loudly, as though he were enjoying himself. Sometimes he sits there by himself for days. Some nights he calls and calls and calls. It sounds very sad. It sounds as if he were crying because he hasn't any friends.

When summer comes, the young raccoons start their schooling. They go to night school. Their mother is the teacher.

She takes her children down to the pond. There she teaches them to look about at the water's edge and to look under the rocks. She waddles about, sniffs, moves little rocks, and tilts up big ones.

The young raccoons are very inquisitive. They rush over and look underneath the rocks. Sometimes they find things; sometimes they don't. They might find a nice fat worm or a crayfish.

If they are lucky, they might even catch a frog. But, best of all, they have learned a way of finding a meal for themselves.

Then comes the lesson in woodcraft. The mother raccoon teaches her children how to find food in the fields and in the forest. She breaks some bark off an old rotten log. The young raccoons rush in and grab the grubs and the insects that are scurrying about. Soon they themselves are breaking away pieces of bark and wood.

If they are lucky, they might even catch a mouse in the old log. They have learned another way of finding a meal for themselves.

The lesson in the treetops is most exciting. There are insects to be had there and spiders. There are nests with eggs. If the young raccoons are lucky, they may even find a squirrel's nest with seeds and nuts, and perhaps the squirrel, too.

When school is over for the night, the mother raccoon teaches her pups how to curl up in a hawk's nest or to stretch out along a limb and go to sleep for the day.

When night comes, the mother skunk takes her little ones out for instruction. She is a fine berry-picker. She is an excellent bug-catcher. She is a splendid mouser.

She teaches all these things to her children. She teaches them how to gather a mouthful of insects at one lick. It looks easy, but it isn't. She

teaches them how to catch a mouse. That is not an easy thing to do, either.

Passers-by do not interrupt these lessons— unless they are very hungry or very foolish. They just ignore the skunks and move along.

If a stroller pauses too long, the mother skunk stamps her front feet; first one, then the other. It means "Move along!" If the stranger still loiters, she raises her tail. That is the final warning. Then she sprays him.

From then on he smells dreadful. When he returns home, his family moves out. Nobody can live with him after one whiff.

In summer, the time for schooling, some animals teach their children to be brave and to fight. Others teach them to be nimble. Some punish them for any misbehavior; others encourage them with kindness.

The woodchuck teaches her children to run away. She uses a whistle to do it. "Don't let trouble catch up with you" is her motto.

When the mother woodchuck emerges after her long winter sleep, she is very watchful. If an enemy appears, she whistles and runs down into her den. If the enemy follows, she fills up the passageway with dirt. She is a fine digger. In this way she shuts a door in the enemy's face.

The mother woodchuck never wanders far from her den. When she has eaten all the grasses near it, she digs a passageway to another feeding place. In so doing, she builds many tunnels.

Her children scamper in and out of them. Every time she builds a new tunnel, she leads her children through it and repeats the lesson she taught them at the other tunnels. She teaches them to run down promptly when she whistles.

She learned this lesson from her own mother and she teaches it to all her children. Every other woodchuck in the country learned the same lesson.

It is their way of life. When a woodchuck sees an enemy and whistles, every woodchuck within hearing, big and small, young and old, runs. That is why we still have woodchucks today.

Summertime is schooltime for the young birds, too. The parents teach them to care for themselves.

The robin wants her children to learn to pull worms out of the ground for themselves. The swallow wants her children to learn to catch bugs for themselves. The woodpecker wants her children to learn to hollow out a home for themselves. Every bird wants her children to learn to be independent.

Often the little birds refuse to go to school.
They stand on the edge of the nest, look down,
and squeak. They are afraid. They wrap their
wings around themselves, pull their heads down
into their shoulders, shut their eyes, and shiver.
The higher the nest is above the ground, the
more they shiver.

The young eagle has the worst time of all on the first day of school. He won't fly. He stands on the edge of the nest and spreads his wings, but he won't take off.

He lives on top of a cliff, and it goes straight down and down and down. Little trees and bushes grow in its crevices—but suppose he misses the trees and tumbles down and down, hundreds and hundreds of feet, and crashes on the bottom on the hard rocks and boulders!

He pulls his big head in between his little shoulders, and shrieks.

The mother eagle circles above the nest and calls to him. The father flies around with a morsel of food in his talons and invites his son to come out for it.

The young eagle looks down those dizzy depths and shivers.

Suddenly the mother eagle lets out a blood-curdling scream and swoops down on her child. Before he can rush back, she strikes the edge of the nest on which he is standing and sweeps him out into the air, clear of the falling sticks.

This is a very dangerous moment in the life of any bird. Will he hold his wings tightly around himself and shiver or will he spread them and flap? Will he struggle for his life in time, or will he give up hope and crash against the rocks below?

As the eaglet falls and flaps through the air, the father eagle calls to him. The father wants him to know that help is at hand. He hopes that this will give the little fellow courage.

The mother eagle flies around, too, and calls to him. She, too, wants to lend him courage until his own develops. She swoops under him when-

ever he is falling too fast, and lets him cling for
a moment on her back. But each time it is just
for a moment; soon he is on his own again, falling and flapping through the air, but each time
with a little more confidence.

The eagles are wise teachers.

Autumn

Autumn is the season of plenty.

The fruits ripen. The nuts fall. There is an abundance of food.

The birds and the animals prepare for the hard times of winter. The birds that fly south eat until they have enough strength for the trip. The animals that remain behind fill their homes with plenty. Those that sleep through the winter fill themselves until they are so full there will be no need to wake up for any more food during the cold months.

The fruits display their best colors. The apples have red cheeks. The pears turn to gold. The grapes take on a deep purple. Every kind of fruit looks its best.

The autumn winds blow the fruit off the trees. It lies all over the ground. Everywhere, some animal or bird is feasting on it.

The nuts break out of their outer shells and drop to the ground. There are chestnuts and hazelnuts and acorns and hickory nuts and butter-nuts and walnuts and other kinds of nuts. There are many varieties of each kind. They lie all over the ground. Everywhere some animal or bird is feasting on them.

The leaves on the trees are beautiful shades of red and gold and brown. They, too, look their best before the autumn winds tear them down and blow them into heaps.

Billions of leaves fall to the ground. The animals move millions of them into their homes for mattresses or to keep out the cold. Millions of leaves remain on the ground like a blanket, to keep it warm.

The fields are covered with fall flowers. Many of them are honey flowers, full of nectar and pollen. It is the autumn honey flow. The bees ramble over these plants and gather the nectar.

Everywhere there is plenty. Food may be had for the taking.

Seeds break out of their coats. They are of all sizes and shapes. As many as a million seeds grow on some plants. Everywhere there are plenty of them. The winds blow them about until it looks as if the whole world is full of seeds. Everywhere

the animals and the birds are feasting on them.

The animals that will sleep over the winter spend the autumn eating. They feed on the fruits and the nuts and the seeds and the grains until they are full. They eat until they cannot eat any more. The others fill their homes with stores of food.

The birds that fly south gather in flocks in the trees and on the fields and over the marshlands. The air is filled with them. It is very gay and exciting. Birds from the north are about to sail over land and sea to the south.

The ducks and the geese and the hawks and the other large birds fly by day. They rise on an updraft until they reach a layer of air moving southward. Then they get aboard this air liner and are carried along by it.

The smaller birds fly by night. They wait until

the airways are clear of big birds. They, too, ride the wind. It takes them south in the autumn and north again in the spring. In this manner they migrate. They roam with the wind from the wilds of the north to the far south.

As they ride along on an air current, they call to each other and their cheeps and trills float down in the quiet of the autumn air.

The birds that migrate in the autumn leave behind some very desirable homes. The owl, who had a good apartment in the trunk of a tree, gives it up. The flickers and the woodpeckers, who lived in an old limb, move out. The hawks, who had a home made of twigs and leaves in the tree-tops, abandon it. The larks leave their good homes of grasses and weeds on the ground in the meadows. There are vacancies everywhere.

The mice in the meadows creep through the

grasses and peek into the empty nests. They are house hunting.

A meadow mouse needs a home every time she has a new litter. Every month, generally, she has about ten new little babies. Before these babies are grown-up, she has another family and

needs a new home again. The ten new babies will grow up and will need ten new homes and will have a hundred children of their own, who will soon need a hundred new homes for a thousand babies, who will soon need a thousand new homes for ten thousand new babies. It takes a lot of empty nests to provide so many mice with homes.

Those that can't find a home ready-made build one of their own.

The mice that live in the trees scramble over the limbs and peek into every tree nest. They, too, are house hunting. They are called white-footed mice, because of their coloring. They move into abandoned bird homes up in the trees and fix them over in mouse style. Then they fill them with food. They run up the weeds and break open the seedcases. They gather thousands of seeds and pack them into their nests.

The chipmunk, too, collects seeds in the autumn, as well as nuts, and carts them down into his den. He brings them down by the mouthful. He crams his mouth so full that his cheeks bulge out almost to his shoulders.

He packs these provisions into his storerooms and into his bedroom under his mattress of leaves and litter, until the seeds and the nuts under the mattress push it up to the ceiling.

The chipmunk goes on collecting seeds and nuts even after his home is full. He stores the extra food near his den, under rocks or beneath bushes. Then he settles down for a nice vacation. He will soon have nothing to do but sleep and eat.

In the autumn the squirrels search for a ready-made home. They scramble about looking for a good one. One home, though, is not enough for a squirrel; he needs three or even four. He needs a home to move to when he has eaten the provisions on hand. He needs another to hide in when enemies are on his track. He needs other homes as storerooms for seeds and nuts and other winter supplies.

If he cannot find an unoccupied hollow tree, the squirrel will search the treetops for an empty hawk's nest. He fixes it over in squirrel style, with snug walls and a good roof. He fills it with seeds and nuts. If he has collected more seeds and nuts than his nest can hold, he buries the rest under the trees.

The woodchuck comes up out of his hole at sunrise every day and starts to eat. He eats everything in sight, fruits and vegetables and melons

and grains and grasses and leaves and stems. He
eats until he is weary and then he goes down for
a nap.

He comes up again at noon for lunch, and
again he eats everything in sight. Again he eats
until he is weary and then he stretches out in the

sunshine for a nap. When he awakens in the late
afternoon, he eats again. Once more he eats until
he is weary and then he goes down to bed.

All he does all through the autumn is eat and
sleep and eat again. By the end of the season he
has eaten so much he cannot eat another thing.

Then he lies down in his den and falls asleep and sleeps so soundly that he doesn't wake up until the next year.

Autumn is a busy season for the beaver. He must gather a woodpile large enough to last all winter. He will need enough for himself and for his mate and for the kits. They feed on wood. They eat just the bark. A beaver family can eat a pile thirty feet square.

So in the autumn the beaver selects his provisions for the winter. He bites a deep groove all around a tree and a second groove about four inches below the first. Then he splits out the wood between the two grooves. He does this with his big strong front teeth. When he has split out the wood between the two grooves, the tree falls.

Beavers are very fond of birch trees. Birch bark,

to them, is very tasty. They also like aspens and poplars and willows.

When the tree is down, the beaver trims it and cuts it into convenient lengths. He drags these pieces out into the pond and makes piles of them under the water near his cabin. If the pieces start to float away, he pushes them into the mud. If they still will not hold, he puts rocks on top of them.

When the pond freezes over, his provisions are under the ice and stay fresh.

In the autumn the bear spends his time eating. He must fill up before winter comes. He likes meat best, but if that is not to be had he will eat what he can get.

When he smells mice in the meadows, he hunts mice. Sometimes, in his hurry to fill up, he gulps the mouse, the nest, and all the seeds and nuts in it. If he scoops up some earth too, he crunches that in the same mouthful.

He digs the chipmunks and the woodchucks out of their dens and dines on them. He digs after them as they try to escape along their tunnels, and snarls and roars and woofs each time they slip away from under his big slapping paw. He digs so hard and so deep that he leaves big empty pits hehind him.

As he woofs and snarls and roars, he can be heard a half mile away. All the little animals within hearing try to hide. They know that a big hungry bear is coming.

Nothing in his path is safe. He gobbles down crickets and ants and grasshoppers. If he finds a nest of hornets or yellow jackets, he swallows them. When he passes a pond, he slaps the bull-frogs out. He is very fond of frogs' legs.

He sits in the orchard for days and feeds on the fruit. When the ground is clear of fallen fruit, he climbs the trees and shakes down more. He likes nuts. He robs squirrels' nests to get them. If the squirrel is at home, he eats him, too. He swallows everything in one gulp.

He tears down big branches from the oaks and the other nut trees, and bites off mouthfuls of nuts and twigs and bark, and crunches them all together.

He likes honey best of all. If he finds a hive or a honey tree, he rips it apart and swallows the comb and the honey and the bees, all at the same time.

By the end of autumn he is well filled.

Winter

Winter is the season for rest.

The little animals creep into snug holes and go to sleep. The bigger animals lie down in sheltered spots and rest.

The roots under the earth put on a coating. The leaf buds cover themselves with scales.

The snail grows a curtain over the doorway to his shell.

The bees in their hive huddle together into clusters.

They all rest. The work of the year is finished.

Spring, the season for babies, is over; summer, the season for learning, is gone; autumn, the season for feasting, is past.

Now it is winter. All life is at rest.

The sun rises later and sets earlier. There is less sunshine, and so there is less heat. The earth cools, and the cold penetrates the ground. Living things try to get away from this cold. They seek warmth. They look for shelter.

Some creep into snug holes. Earthworms dig down. Often they dig down as much as six feet and farther. There they hollow out little chambers. Earthworms by the dozen cluster in these chambers for warmth and rest. Every worm that can squeeze in does so.

The digger wasp makes a burrow and fills it with provisions. She stores up cicadas and spiders

and flies and other delicacies. Then she lays some eggs. When the young hatch out, lunch is ready for them.

The queen bumblebees dig under the ground for the winter. So, too, do the queens of the paper-making wasps, and other female insects. Their males are all dead; when the cold weather came, they died off.

The survival of the species depends on these buried queens. If they do not freeze during the winter, they can lay eggs again and have offspring to continue the race. If they select safe winter quarters, the world will again be blessed with wasps and bumblebees.

The surface of the earth hardens as it cools. In time, it freezes so hard that no more cold can get through. The hard crust on top protects the living things underneath.

Life settles down to rest. Everything is quiet. The sounds of other seasons are heard no longer.

There are no leaves on the trees to rustle in the wind.

The songbirds have gone south. The honeybees and the bumblebees and the bugs that once buzzed around are quiet. The frogs and the toads that once filled the air with their calls are asleep in the mud.

A cover of ice silences the murmuring brook, and the waterfall hangs motionless.

The sound heard most often now is the wild winter wind blowing over the ice and snow.

Everything is glad to turn in and rest.

For many living things a tree is home in the wintertime. It is the biggest apartment house in nature.

Strings of katydid eggs hang from it, and nests

rest in its branches. Bugs and beetles dwell under its bark. Caterpillars that will one day change into beautiful moths spin cocoons onto twigs, and then spin themselves into them for their long winter nap. Honeybees fill the hollow trunk with a hundred thousand young. Every pocket in the tree is a home for some living thing.

Some tenants stay on in their tree home only if the winter season is not too severe. They are not afraid of winter weather, but they don't want too much of it.

The great horned owl is one of these. He is not afraid of snow or ice or cold. But when the sharp frosts have frozen all the waters in the far north, and the winds scream across the mountains and tear down great trees, and the blizzards cover everything with piled-up snow, the great horned owl and his mate seek a more temperate spot.

They move down from the far north till they come to snow fields that are not constantly whipped up by the winds. There they settle if they can find a tree that just rocks in the wind, without blowing away. There they pass the winter, sliding down the snowdrifts and whipping up the snowflakes. It is good fun.

The great horned owl has many relatives and neighbors in the far north. There is the snowy

owl, a big white bird, and the arctic owl and the great gray owl and others. They are colored like the countrysides in which they live. They look like little snow piles sticking up out of bigger snow piles. When the gales and the blizzards become unbearable, they also move southward. When the snow falls they, too, frolic in the snowflakes.

In the far north, masses of ice split off from

their mother glacier. In pieces as big as a mountain top they move down the ice slide and crash into the sea. Now they are icebergs, one ninth above water and eight ninths below.

Ravens perch on the new iceberg and seals in the water near it dash about until the mass of ice steadies itself before the driving winds and the sea currents.

The wind howls. The ravens scream back at the wind. But their voices, that once could make a polar bear turn tail and flee, have no effect on the wind; it blows just as hard as ever and tears from the icebergs the perches that had attracted the ravens.

So the ravens, too, are finally driven southward for the winter. Some fly to high cliffs overlooking the ocean; others select big trees in the forest. There they perch and rest.

106

The smaller birds are not so hardy as the bigger ones. They do not stay in the far north until the blizzards drive them out. At the approach of winter many of them ride to the warm south on the airways.

Others come down from the far north but do not travel all the way to a warm place. Among these are crows and jays and chickadees and juncos and hawks and sparrows. They are used to trees trimmed in snow and icicles.

The jays flutter on and off the snow-packed limbs. The hawks swoop after them, and the crows perch on top of the trees and scream.

Chickadees twitter and twirl on the snowy twigs, and the nuthatches walk upside down on the underside of the branches. When it is very cold, they swell out their feathers, and the fluffy down underneath ruffles up. This thickens their covering and keeps out the cold.

When it becomes too chilly, they are very uncomfortable. They huddle and hunch and shiver, and finally they leave for a place that is farther south.

By wintertime the bears, too, are ready for a rest. All summer long they played with the babies. It kept them very busy. All autumn long they ate. They ate enough to put on a solid layer of fat, four inches thick. Over the fat they grew a thick coat of oily hair. The fat will keep out the cold. The coat will shed the sleet and the rain.

The bears look about for a place to tuck in and sleep.

The polar bear gets into an ice cave or a snow-drift. The bear on the mountain side backs in under a ledge of rock. The bear in the woodland looks for a hollow tree.

Then they tuck in and sleep through the win-ter. The snow piles up around the entrance way

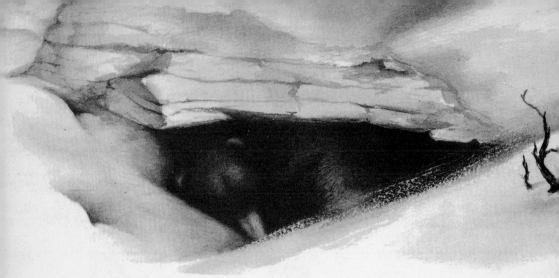

and keeps out the wind and the cold. It is a comfortable way to spend a winter.

Sometimes a bear cannot find an unoccupied niche. In that case, he scrapes out a hollow alongside a fallen tree, which serves as a windbreak, or under its roots. He lines it with leaves and grasses and turns in. As he sleeps, the storms pile a blanket of snow on top of him. The more it snows, the thicker grows the blanket. The snow hides him from enemies while he sleeps. The windbreak keeps the wind from blowing his blanket away.

The rabbit does not tuck in and sleep for the winter as the bear does. Too many eyes are looking for him; too many noses are sniffing around to find him. Snow often melts on the warmer winter days, and then the animal underneath shows through.

The bear is safe at such times because he wakes up and growls. His growl warns prowlers who hoped for a taste of bear that he is awake and prepared to exchange bites.

The rabbit does not tuck in. He hides under a bush or in the brush or under a tree whose limbs hang low over the ground. If he is lucky, he has

a hollow log or a woodchuck's abandoned den for blizzard weather.

If he sees enemy eyes looking for him or hears enemy noses sniffing for him, he sits as motionless as the ground that holds him. Just his whiskers tremble a little. When enemies discover him, he runs.

At night he creeps out of his hiding place and looks for food. He must do this or go hungry. If it rains or snows when he wants a meal, he must go out for it in the rain or snow. He did not eat enough in the autumn to carry him through the winter; neither did he stock food for a rainy day.

There is not so much to select from in the wintertime, perhaps some dried-up grasses or some old briers or some bark off a tree trunk. Still, that is better than nothing.

So the rabbit goes out of his hiding place at night and feeds on whatever he can find. His long ears stand up at attention, ready to receive any warning sound. His big strong legs are ready to run.

The rabbit's world is full of enemies. Yet he has something to be thankful for in the wintertime; his enemies rest more, and so he can, too.

By the time winter comes, the raccoon is very tired. He has been up and down trees all year. He has been up to their very tops and out to the very ends of the branches after birds and eggs. He has fished, dug for mice, feasted on grubs, berried, sneaked into the farmer's garden, and robbed his henroost.

He has lived well. These delicacies have put fat on his ribs. Every bug, every frog, every melon and ear of corn have added to his weight. By wintertime, he is dragging more weight up the trees, and more weight is pushing him down.

Once, if he wanted to, he could go down the tree headfirst like a squirrel. He seldom dares to do that now; his extra weight pushes and shoves from above till his legs ache and his nails ache more from the effort to save himself from tumbling down.

116

Now, by wintertime, he is very tired and ready for a rest. So he looks about for a hollow in a tree.

When he finds one, he moves in for the winter with his fat mate. If there is room, he permits his fat children to move in, too. If there is still room, he is joined by his fat father and his fat mother and their parents, too; that is, if they haven't been eaten yet by a hungry wolf.

There they will all rest until warmer nights return.

When wintertime comes, the fox has nothing to do but eat and keep warm. He trots over to the sunny side of a hill, fits himself into a hollow, and wraps his tail around himself. He naps with one eye open and watches for a passing meal.

Other hungry hunters are doing the very same thing at the very same time. Sometimes an owl swoops down first and carries the prize away.

Sometimes the owl and the fox pounce at the same prey at the same moment. Then the meal escapes and the owl and the fox end up biting and scratching each other.

When a meal is not to be had by waiting for it, the fox goes hunting.

He likes mice, but he can't locate a mouse unless it squeaks, and it won't squeak until he locates it. He likes pheasant, but they whirr out of the snow and away.

He likes young beaver. But even though he has one right under his nose, he can't scratch through the ice which has locked the beaver into the pond and himself out of it.

So although the fox hasn't much to do in the wintertime except eat, there isn't much he can get to eat. His stomach gets a good deal of rest.

When the winter weather is at its coldest, the

mouse drops off to sleep. She may sleep all day or a week or several weeks. She has worked hard all year and she is tired. She has cut grass stems down and built runways between her nest and the meadows. She has trucked hundreds of thousands of seeds from the meadows to her nest.

By wintertime, the nest is stocked with a fortune in food. She has goodies of all sorts: quarts of clover seeds and dandelion roots and nuts and berry seeds and other delicacies.

She has worked every night of the week, every week of the summer and autumn to gather them.

In addition, she has brought several families into the world and fed and raised them. She should be tired now and stay at home and rest.

She should be mindful that almost every bird and almost every animal that is up and about now is very hungry, and on the watch for a mouse.

But the mouse is a restless little animal. Between naps she nibbles. Then she rushes out to gather seeds to replace the little she has consumed. Up and down the naked stems she clambers to harvest the seeds that remain on top.

Enemy eyes are ever on the lookout for such a morsel.

Back home her storehouse is full of the good food she has saved. Had she stayed at home she could have feasted and stayed fat and sweet. Instead, she ventures forth and leaves her hoard at home unprotected, and risks being captured.

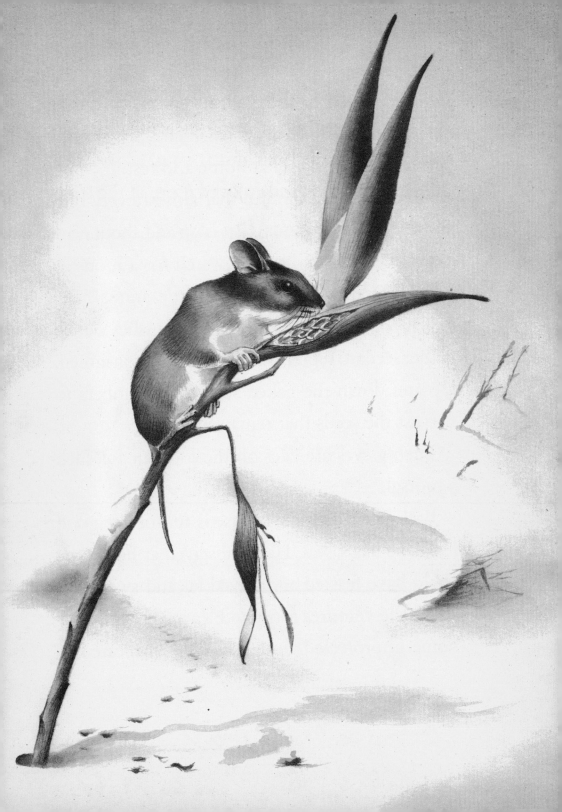

Whoever gets her will be satisfied with her as she is, however. He will never know that his meal would have been much sweeter had that little mouse rested and enjoyed more of the fruits of her own labor.

This has been the story of the four seasons: spring, summer, autumn, and winter. Each one is different from the others. For that reason the animals and the birds acted differently in each of them.

In the spring they fixed up a home and had babies. In the summer they taught their children to care for themselves. In the autumn they filled themselves or their homes with food. In the winter they rested.

When spring returns, they will be ready to start the work of the year again. Unless, in the meanwhile, someone eats them up.

DATE DUE

NOV 9 '85			
			PRINTED IN U.S.A.
GAYLORD			